# Summer Lea

## Preparation for Grade 4

**Grades 3-4**

**Written by Melanie Komar**
**Illustrated by S&S Learning Materials**

**ISBN 1-55035-786-7**

**Revised January 2006**
 "We acknowledge the financial support of the Government of Canada through the Book Publishing Industry Development Program (BPIDP) for this project."

Published in the United States by:
On the Mark Press
3909 Witmer Road PMB 175
Niagara Falls, New York
14305
www.onthemarkpress.com

Published in Canada by:
S&S Learning Materials
15 Dairy Avenue
Napanee, Ontario
K7R 1M4
www.sslearning.com

## Additional Hands-On Activities

This is just a sample of activities that children can do with an adult or older child. Do only as much as the child is capable of, remembering that all children develop certain skills at different times. Some of the activities are strictly for enjoyment, while others may reinforce skills that the child has learned, but all activities should be done strictly for the enjoyment of learning.

1. Make a calendar for each month of the summer. Decorate each one with pictures you have drawn or cut out from magazines. Keep track of special days, outings, or anything else that you feel is important.
2. Read every day. Participate in a library reading program. Set a goal for yourself, to read a number of books over the summer.
3. Go bird watching.
4. Start a journal and record everything that you do through the summer.
5. Make a zoo, using construction paper to make all of the animals that you think are in a zoo.
6. Sign out a science book from the library and try some of the experiments.
7. Get together with your friends and go bicycle riding.
8. Take a trip with your family to the Farmer's Market. Learn about the fruits and vegetables that are grown in your area. Then, after you have bought some of the fresh produce, take them home and incorporate them into a healthy lunch.
9. Take a camera with you on your vacation. When the pictures are developed, add them to your journal.
10. Make a musical instrument. Get together with others your own age and put together a band using your home-made instruments.
11. Make up a list of items for your own scavenger hunt. Descriptions can include things like "round and yellow", or "octagonal and red and white", or "square and brown". Then take a walk and look for the things described on your list.
12. Organize a "Neighborhood Olympics". Get together with all of your friends and play games for the day.
13. Make a calendar and track the weather for a whole month, using picture symbols to tell the weather. At the end of the month, count the number of days for each kind of weather.
14. Make your own list of books that you would like to read.
15. Plant your own garden, with vegetables or flowers, or a combination of both.
16. Make a map of your neighborhood.
17. Put on an exhibit of the crafts that you made during the summer for your family and friends.
18. Take up kite flying.
19. Start a collection: rocks, pressed flowers, feathers - whatever you like.
20. Go berry picking. Then, with an adult, make something good out of the berries that you have picked.
21. Attend outdoor concerts at your local park. Take along a blanket and a picnic and enjoy!
22. Discover the joy of Nature Walks and take along a magnifying glass or binoculars.
23. Sleep under the stars and identify the constellations and stars that you see in the sky.
24. Pack a lunch and a ball or Frisbee and go to the park for an afternoon of fun.

# Alphabetical Order

LANGUAGE

In your neatest cursive writing, rewrite these words in alphabetical order:

1. serf, nobleman, knight, king, peasant, viking

_______________________________________________

_______________________________________________

2. carnivore, food, omnivore, predator, herbivore, decomposer, ecosystem

_______________________________________________

_______________________________________________

3. hospital, school, library, synagogue, store, police, bakery, office

_______________________________________________

_______________________________________________

# Addition and Subtraction Review

MATHEMATICS

| | | | | |
|---|---|---|---|---|
| a) 34 <br> + 44 | b) 67 <br> + 23 | c) 45 <br> + 27 | d) 89 <br> - 63 | e) 21 <br> - 10 |
| f) 128 <br> + 351 | g) 634 <br> + 255 | h) 523 <br> + 376 | i) 352 <br> - 241 | j) 920 <br> - 710 |
| k) 467 <br> - 132 | l) 753 <br> - 253 | m) 490 <br> - 439 | n) 234 <br> + 427 | o) 264 <br> - 172 |
| p) 435 <br> + 336 | q) 876 <br> + 147 | r) 845 <br> + 127 | s) 933 <br> - 634 | t) 354 <br> + 455 |

LANGUAGE

## Root Words, Prefixes and Suffixes

Write the **root word**, the **prefix** and the **suffix** of each word below. Note: Some of these words have a prefix, some have a suffix, and some have both a prefix and a suffix. The first one has been done for you.

1. busiest ➡ **busy + est**
2. mighty ➡ ______________
3. earlier ➡ ______________
4. unhappy ➡ ______________
5. action ➡ ______________
6. retell ➡ ______________
7. snoring ➡ ______________
8. lefty ➡ ______________
9. unfriendly ➡ ______________
10. prettier ➡ ______________

MATHEMATICS

## Sequencing Numbers

**1.** Count up. Write the missing numbers.

**a)** 6, 7, 8, ____, ____, ____, ____, ____, ____, ____, 16

**b)** 71, 72, 73, ____, ____, ____, ____, ____, ____, ____, 81

**c)** 124, 125, 126, ____, ____, ____, ____, ____, ____, 133

**d)** 6 234, 6 235, 6 236, ____, ____, ____, ____, ____, 6 242

**e)** 1 095, 1 096, 1 097, ____, ____, ____, ____, ____, 1 103

**2.** Count down. Write the missing numbers.

**a)** 13, 12, 11, ____, ____, ____, ____, ____, ____, ____, 3

**b)** 45, 44, 43, ____, ____, ____, ____, ____, ____, ____, 35

**c)** 721, 720, 719, ____, ____, ____, ____, ____, ____, ____, 711

**d)** 4 323, 4 322, 4 321, ____, ____, ____, ____, ____, 4 315

**e)** 2 095, 2 094, 2 093, ____, ____, ____, ____, ____, 2 087

# The Medieval Times

SOCIAL STUDIES

Imagine living in the medieval times! That was a time when there were far less people living in the world. Nobody moved away from the town where they were born. There was no electricity, no cars, no water from a tap, no refrigerators, no video games, no computers or televisions.

Match the descriptions of people with the pictures below to learn about some of the kinds of people who lived in the medieval times. Print the letter of the correct description beside the matching picture.

**a)** Monks (men) ate simple food, dressed in simple clothes (called habits) and spent their days in silence, praying or working.

**b)** A **knight** had many pounds of armor that he had to wear to protect himself from the arrows and swords of enemies.

**c)** Nuns (women) ate simple food, dressed in simple clothes (called habits) and spent their days in silence, praying or working.

**d)** A **king** ruled all the people who lived in his kingdom. He had a variety of expensive clothes, and often wore a crown and brightly colored silks.

**1.**

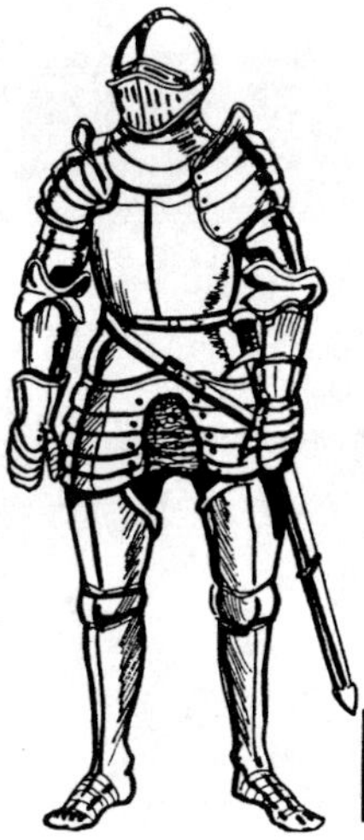

**2.**

**3.**

**4.**

MATHEMATICS

# Least to Greatest, Greatest to Least

Put these numbers in order from **least** to **greatest**.

a) 35 87 92 45 ➡ ______ ______ ______ ______

b) 234 549 344 602 ➡ ______ ______ ______ ______

c) 756 346 975 106 ➡ ______ ______ ______ ______

d) 573 590 523 564 ➡ ______ ______ ______ ______

e) 212 217 216 210 ➡ ______ ______ ______ ______

Put these numbers in order from **greatest** to **leastest**.

f) 45 85 46 90 ➡ ______ ______ ______ ______

g) 487 934 547 651 ➡ ______ ______ ______ ______

h) 875 450 231 734 ➡ ______ ______ ______ ______

i) 657 690 634 651 ➡ ______ ______ ______ ______

j) 877 874 875 870 ➡ ______ ______ ______ ______

LANGUAGE

# Prefixes and Suffixes

Add the **prefixes** and **suffixes** to each root word below.

1. un + kind = ____________________
2. friendly + est = ____________________
3. re + call = ____________________
4. long + er = ____________________
5. beauty + ful = ____________________
6. un + lucky = ____________________
7. happy + er = ____________________
8. re + act + ion = ____________________
9. memory + ies = ____________________
10. dis + like = ____________________
11. nice + est = ____________________
12. discuss + ion = ____________________

MATHEMATICS

## Addition - With an Unknown Term

The letter **n** stands for an **unknown**. To solve for n, figure out which number belongs where the n is. The first one has been done for you.

| | | | | | |
|---|---|---|---|---|---|
| **a)** **3 + 4 = n** | ➡ | **n = 7** | **b)** 6 + 4 = n | ➡ | ________ |
| **c)** 5 + 3 = n | ➡ | ________ | **d)** 7 + 7 = n | ➡ | ________ |
| **e)** n = 4 + 1 | ➡ | ________ | **f)** 8 + 5 = n | ➡ | ________ |
| **g)** n = 6 + 5 | ➡ | ________ | **h)** 7 + 3 = n | ➡ | ________ |
| **i)** 8 + 4 = n | ➡ | ________ | **j)** 9 + 4 = n | ➡ | ________ |
| **k)** n = 4 + 4 | ➡ | ________ | **l)** 6 + 6 = n | ➡ | ________ |
| **m)** 3 + 2 + 5 = n | ➡ | ________ | **n)** 3 + 4 + 4 = n | ➡ | ________ |
| **o)** n = 4 + 5 + 5 | ➡ | ________ | **p)** 5 + 3 + 3 = n | ➡ | ________ |

LANGUAGE

## Making Nouns Plural

Write the **plural** of the word in brackets on the line.

1. The (**shelf**) ________________ are filled with books.
2. The eagle brought food for her (**baby**) ________________.
3. How many (**fox**) ________________ chased the rabbit?
4. The (**child**) ________________ learned about pioneers.
5. The (**mouse**) ________________ scampered into their hole.
6. The frog caught some (**fly**) ________________.
7. The squirrel found nuts under the (**leaf**) ________________.
8. Some herbivores eat (**berry**) ________________.
9. The bees made a hive in the (**bush**) ________________.
10. Two (**wolf**) ________________ ran after the sheep.

READING

# Reading for Understanding - The Food Chain

Read the following information about the food chain. Then answer the questions below. You may need to use the internet, the library or areas around your home to research the answers to some of the questions.

**Plants** are very important to the food chain. Some things in the food chain live in plants (for example, squirrels live in trees); other things in the food chain use parts of plants (twigs, grass, leaves, etc.) to build their homes. Everything in the food chain either eats plants or eats things that eat plants. Plants need sunlight and water to grow and live.

A **habitat** is a community of plants and animals. It is where animals get their food and water; it's where they live. Whether you live in a rural town or a bustling city, there is a habitat in your own yard!

**Animals** that only eat plants are called herbivores (example: cows). Animals that eat only meat are called carnivores (example: wolves). Animals that eat both plants and meat are called omnivores (example: bears). Prey are animals that are hunted (example: rabbits). Predators are animals that hunt (example: hawks). Some animals are both prey and predators (example: snakes).

1. What do plants need to grow? ______________________________

2. Why are plants so important?

   ______________________________________________________

3. An animal that eats only plants is called a ____________________. Two examples of plant-eaters are ____________________ and ____________________.

4. Meat-eaters are called ____________________. Two examples of meat-eaters are ____________________ and ____________________.

5. An omnivore eats ____________________ and ____________________. Are you an omnivore? ______________

READING

6. Describe a habitat.

______________________________

______________________________

7. You have a habitat in your yard. Go outside where you live and list some living things that you see. Include plants, insects and animals. Think about things that you have seen there before but may not be there now (for example, birds, spiders, dandelions) and list those, also.

______________________________

______________________________

______________________________

8. Are there any plants in your yard's habitat that were not planted by anyone? If so, how did they get there? Are there any animals (living creatures) that you did not put there? If so, how did they get there?

______________________________

______________________________

______________________________

9. What is prey? ______________________________

10. Name two examples of prey. ______________________________

11. What is a predator? ______________________________

12. Name two examples of predators. ______________________________

13. Think about what each living thing below eats. Then, write "**prey**", "**predator**" or "**both**" beside each creature below. (**Hint**: If an animal is a plant-eater, it is likely prey to a predator.)

**a)** spider ______________ **b)** fox ______________

**c)** frog ______________ **d)** rabbit ______________

**e)** wolf ______________ **f)** sheep ______________

14. What do you think would happen to other living things if there were no plants left on the Earth?

______________________________

______________________________

SCIENCE

# Natural and Artificial Light

There are two types of light: **natural light** and **artifical** light. Natural light is found in objects found in nature. Artificial light can be found in human-made objects.

1. Below each picture write **"n"** for **natural light** or **"a"** for **artificial light**.

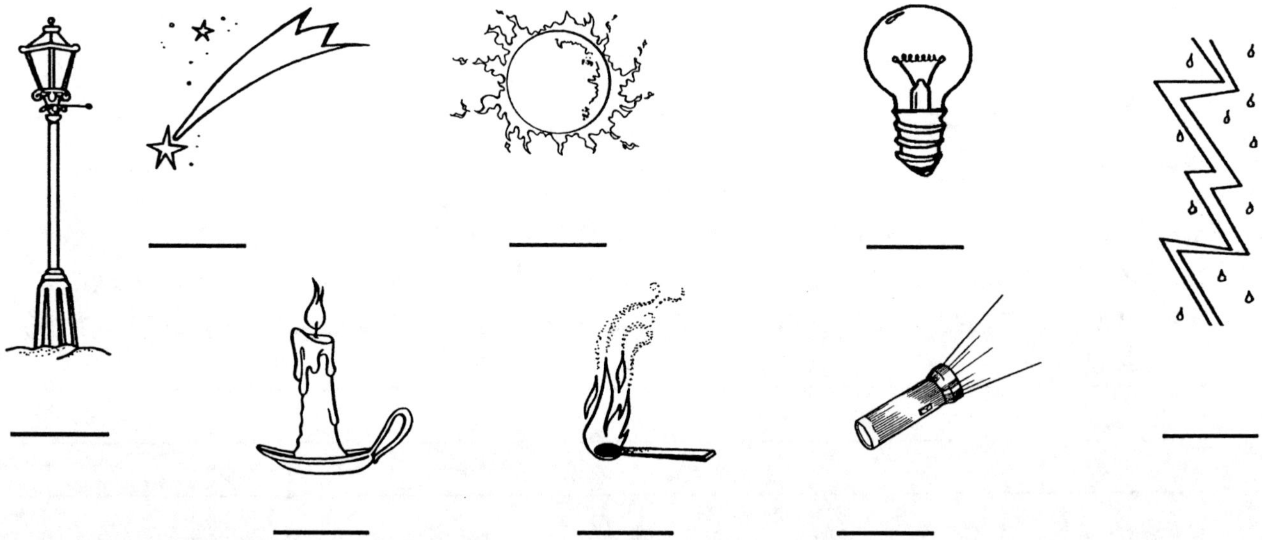

2. Circle the sources of light that humans are able to use.

MATHEMATICS

# Greater Than or Less Than?

Put a **<** or **>** to show if the first number is greater than or less than the second number. The first one has been done for you.

| | |
|---|---|
| **a)** 30 (<) 76 | **b)** 45 ( ) 67 |
| **c)** 80 ( ) 34 | **d)** 21 ( ) 78 |
| **e)** 75 ( ) 76 | **f)** 84 ( ) 48 |
| **g)** 123 ( ) 678 | **h)** 787 ( ) 877 |
| **i)** 934 ( ) 943 | **j)** 344 ( ) 400 |
| **k)** 810 ( ) 890 | **l)** 378 ( ) 387 |

## Alliteration

An **alliteration** is the repeating of the sounds at the beginning of words. **Example:** Sam Smith saved six slithering snakes, so Suzanna started saying silly slogans.

LANGUAGE

Make up two alliterations with any two different letters of the alphabet.

______________________________________________

______________________________________________

______________________________________________

______________________________________________

______________________________________________

How many words in each sentence start with the same letter?

______________________________________________

______________________________________________

## Subtraction - With and Without Regrouping

MATHEMATICS

Solve.

| | | | | |
|---|---|---|---|---|
| a) 78 - 49 | b) 67 - 28 | c) 85 - 26 | d) 31 - 13 | e) 52 - 14 |
| f) 468 - 351 | g) 634 - 255 | h) 573 - 376 | i) 652 - 241 | j) 920 - 711 |
| k) 367 - 238 | l) 463 - 254 | m) 567 - 439 | n) 285 - 137 | o) 243 - 167 |
| p) 535 - 347 | q) 634 - 128 | r) 643 - 154 | s) 901 - 345 | t) 825 - 349 |

SCIENCE

## Characteristics of Plants - Fibrous Roots and Tap Roots

There are two main types of plant roots. **Fibrous roots** have **many branches that spread throughout the soil layers. Tap** roots have one main thick root that grows down into the soil and many smaller roots branching off the main root.

1. Go outside with a garden trowel (or spoon) and paper bags. Look for weeds. (Weeds are plants that are growing in places where they are not wanted.) Carefully dig up different kinds of weeds without disturbing other plants. Make sure you get as much of the roots of the weed as possible. Shake the dirt off the roots and place the weed and attached roots into a paper bag. Collect several weeds with each of the two different kinds of root systems.

2. Once you are back inside, spread out the weeds that you have collected on newspapers or paper towels. Examine their root systems. Sort the weeds that you have collected into those that have fibrous roots and those that have tap roots. On a separate piece of paper, sketch a sample of each kind of root system.

SOCIAL STUDIES

## Urban and Rural Communities

1. Use a dictionary or your grade three school notes to write the definition of the following terms:
   a) urban community: ______________________________
   b) rural community: ______________________________

2. Which type of community do you live in?

   ______________________________

3. Do you know anyone who lives in the other type of community?

   ______________________________

4. What do you think is better about living in a urban community?

   ______________________________

5. What do you think is better about living in a rural community?

   ______________________________

# Community Buildings

Circle the buildings that you would find in an **urban community**. Put a box around the buildings that you would find in a **rural community**.

(**Note:** Some buildings are found in **both** communities.)

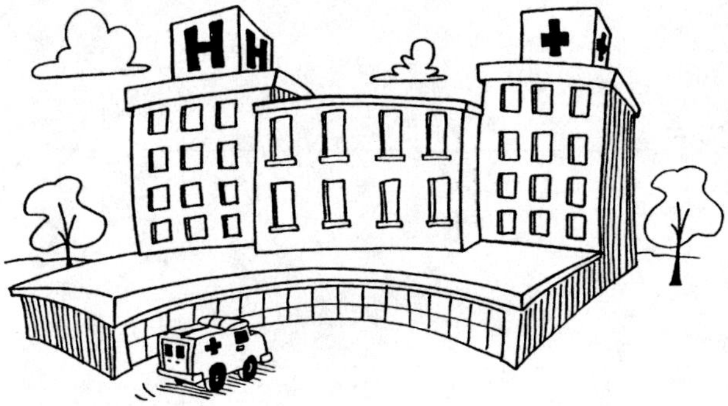

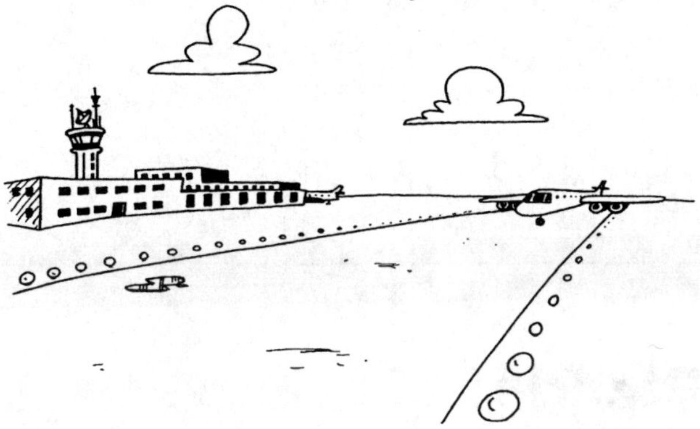

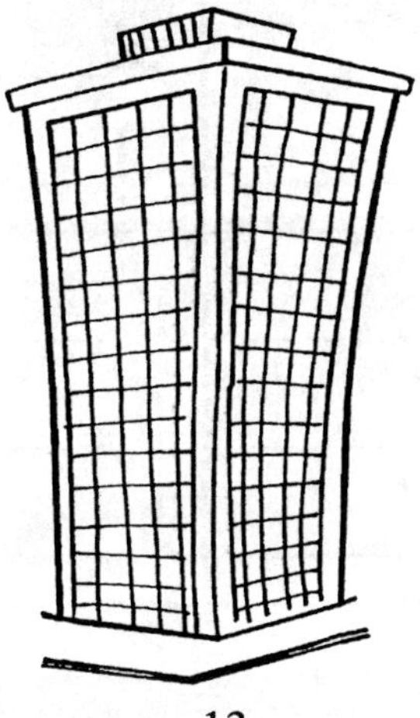

MATHEMATICS

## Addition - With Units of Time

Solve. (**Tip:** You may use a calculator.) Show all your work. The first question has been done for you. Simplify your answer as shown in the example.

a) **2 hours 45 minutes + 4 hours 25 minutes = 7 hours 10 minutes**

2 + 4 = **6 hours**
45 + 25 = **70 minutes**
70 minutes = **1 hour 10 minutes**

b) 4 hours 15 minutes + 5 hours 20 minutes = ______________________

c) 7 weeks 3 days + 2 weeks 4 days = ______________________

d) 2 weeks 4 days 3 hours 50 minutes + 1 week 2 days 7 hours 15 minutes = ______________________

PHONICS

## Consonant Blends

A consonant blend is **two consonants** that make a **new** sound when put together. Write three words that have the following consonant blends in them:

| | | | |
|---|---|---|---|
| gr __________ | st __________ | cl __________ | __________ ck |
| gr __________ | st __________ | cl __________ | __________ ck |
| gr __________ | st __________ | cl __________ | __________ ck |
| tr __________ | cr __________ | fl __________ | __________ sk |
| tr __________ | cr __________ | fl __________ | __________ sk |
| tr __________ | cr __________ | fl __________ | __________ sk |

MATHEMATICS

# Multiplication Facts - Complete the Chart

| X | 0 | 1 | 2 | 3 | 4 | 5 | 6 | 7 | 8 | 9 | 10 | 11 | 12 |
|---|---|---|---|---|---|---|---|---|---|---|---|---|---|
| 1 | | | | | | | | | | | 10 | | |
| 2 | | 2 | | | | | | | | | | | |
| 3 | | | | | | | | | | | | | |
| 4 | | | | | | | | | | | | | |
| 5 | | | | | | 25 | | | | | | | |
| 6 | | | | | | | | | | | | | |
| 7 | 0 | | | | | | | | | | | | |
| 8 | | | | | | | | | | | | | |
| 9 | | | | | | | | | | | | | |
| 10 | | | | 30 | | | | | | | | | |
| 11 | | | | | | | | | 88 | | | | |
| 12 | | | | | | | | | | | | | |

SCIENCE

# Levels of Sound

Sound is measured in **decibels (db)**. The louder a sound is, the more decibels it has. Very loud sounds can cause discomfort, pain or even loss of hearing.

**Normal breathing = 10 db**
**Some discomfort = 90 db**
**Damage to ears = 140 db**
**Normal conversation = 60 db**
**Level of pain = 130 db**

**Circle** the pictures of things that can cause some discomfort, pain or damage.

gas lawnmower = 110 db

telephone = 70 db

loud scream = 115 db

space shuttle = 170 db

bird chirping = 25 db

rock concert = 130 db

many students talking in class = 90 db

LANGUAGE

## Punctuation

**Add** the proper punctuation to these sentences about the medieval times. If a word needs a capital letter, cross off the lower case letter and print the upper case letter above it.

1. there was a pyramid society There were different classes of people such as kings queens lords clerics and peasants
2. peasants worked long hours on farmland owned by a lords manor Men wore coarse tunics Women wore long dresses of coarse wool
3. she looked out the castle window and saw the knight on his horse charging directly towards the castle wall Then she heard a big boom
4. the commoners' houses were made of cement wood and straw
5. ouch exclaimed the cook as the boiling water splashed on his arm
6. the king sniffed the plate of food placed before him and said Mmmm this smells good

MATHEMATICS

## More Multiplication

Solve.

| | | |
|---|---|---|
| a) 3 X 4 = ______ | b) 5 X 6 = ______ | c) 2 X 10 = ______ |
| d) 6 X 7 = ______ | e) 5 X 8 = ______ | f) 7 X 4 = ______ |
| g) 9 X 2 = ______ | h) 4 X 9 = ______ | i) 2 X 3 = ______ |
| j) 4 X 6 = ______ | k) 3 X 6 = ______ | l) 6 X 9 = ______ |
| m) 7 X 8 = ______ | n) 9 X 0 = ______ | o) 8 X 3 = ______ |
| p) 11 X 3 = ______ | q) 4 X 5 = ______ | r) 1 X 6 = ______ |
| s) 9 X 3 = ______ | t) 6 X 4 = ______ | u) 2 X 2 = ______ |

| | | | |
|---|---|---|---|
| v) 3 | w) 5 | x) 0 | y) 9 |
| x 3 | x 3 | x 5 | x 8 |
| ______ | ______ | ______ | ______ |

# Contractions

A contraction is **two words** put together to make **one smaller word**. For example, **"I'll"** is **"I will"**.

__Underline__ the contractions in the sentences below. Then rewrite them in their full form in the space beside each sentence.

1. They'll catch fish for dinner. ______________
2. I think he's going to milk the cow. ______________
3. The king's safe in his castle. ______________
4. I'd like to learn about jungle habitats. ______________
5. The hawk couldn't catch the squirrel. ______________
6. She'll sleep in the guest bedroom. ______________
7. When you're at the concert, do you wear ear plugs? ______________
8. I'm reading a book about King Arthur. ______________
9. Katie said that Ian's not going swimming today. ______________
10. We've started studying the human body at school. ______________

# Possessive Pronouns

A possessive pronoun is a pronoun that **shows ownership**, such as "his".

Circle all the possessive pronouns in the sentences below.

1. "Don't take that. It's mine!"
2. Where is his hamburger?
3. The dolphins were looking for their dinner.
4. We will study for our test.
5. The king wore a crown on his head.
6. That is Rupert's fish.
7. The bear stalked its prey.
8. That looks like your shirt.
9. I put it in my bedroom.
10. She brushed her horse.

SCIENCE

# Growth and Changes in Plants

**1.** Look through magazines, calendars and photographs for pictures of plants. Glue the pictures on a separate piece of paper and write the answers to the following questions.

- **a)** How are these plants different from each other?
- **b)** How are these plants similar to one another?
- **c)** What do you think happens to each plant in the winter?
- **d)** What changes do you think there are in the spring?
- **e)** What would the plants look like in the summer?
- **f)** What happens to these plants in the fall?

**2.** Now, take a notebook and pencil and go for a walk around your yard and neighborhood. In your notebook, draw a picture of some plants that you see. Write their names down if you know them. Describe each plant. Return home when you have found at least five different kinds of plants.

**3.** At home, write down how you think each plant will change next season. Which ones do you think will die before the winter? For the ones that won't die, write down what changes will happen to them.

**4.** Draw how you think each of the trees below will look in the winter.

| Summer | Winter |
|---|---|
|  Fir Tree | |
|  Apple Tree | |

# More Punctuation

Add the proper punctuation to these paragraphs. If a word needs a capital letter, cross off the lower case letter and print the upper case letter above it.

LANGUAGE

in medieval times, kings and queens lived in castles Sometimes the enemy would attack the castle so castles were often built on a mountain with a moat around it A drawbridge lay across the moat to allow friends to get in but the drawbridge would be raised if an enemy came near

castles had an inner wall and an outer wall The outer wall was covered with merlons (steel plates) The walls were very thick to help prevent attackers from breaking them down The walls had small slits called arrow loops Defenders could shoot arrows at the enemy through these slits

# Problem Solving

MATHEMATICS

Answer each question with a proper sentence.

1. Mohammed baked 15 cookies and shared them with 3 children. Each child got the same amount of cookies. How many cookies did each child get?

2. Rebecca spent $9.00 on books. She bought 3 books that each cost the same amount of money. How much did each book cost?

3. The Boston Bears scored the same number of runs during each of the 9 innings of their baseball game. They scored a total of 18 runs. How many runs did they score in each inning?

LANGUAGE

# Identifying Verbs - Present and Past Tense

> Verbs in the **present tense** are actions that are happening now. Verbs in the **past tense** are actions that happened before.

Read the sentences below. **Circle** all the verbs in the **present tense**. **Underline** all the verbs in the **past tense**.

1. Last week, I watched a movie about medieval times.
2. She is waiting for her knight in shining armor.
3. The sly fox waited quietly for his prey.
4. Thomas Edison invented the light bulb.
5. Swimming is fun!
6. Grace plays the harp for the king every evening.
7. When the manta ray swims past, the shark lunges.

MATHEMATICS

# Picture Division

**Divide** the **food** on the left, evenly, to the **predators** on the right by drawing a line from each food to one of the predators. Make sure each predator in the group gets an equal amount of food.

# Reading Comprehension

READING

The desert air was very hot and dry. As the sun was setting, Roady Roadrunner was just waking up in his nest in the shade. It wasn't as hot at night, so he liked to work and play after the sun had set. The other animals were just waking up also, and they were hungry. Roady watched as a mouse nibbled on plant seeds that had fallen to the ground. Nibble, nibble. Suddenly, without warning, a snake slithered over and gobbled up the mouse in one bite!

"Perfect," thought Roady. "Now that the snake is distracted, I'll run over and catch a meal for myself!" And soon, he was feasting on snake for breakfast!

Read the story and answer the questions on a separate sheet of paper.

1. Who is the main character?
2. Where and when does the story take place (setting)?
3. Why do the animals sleep during the day?
4. List four links of the food chain that are found in the story. Put the roadrunner as the first link at the top of the food chain.
5. Do you think this is a realistic story or a fantasy? Why?

# Book Report

Read a fictional book that you have at home, or choose one from the library. Then, answer these questions about it on a separate sheet of paper.

1. **Characters:** a) Who is the main character?
   b) List some other important characters.
2. Setting: Where and when does the story happen?
3. Problem: What is the main conflict in the story?
4. Evaluation: Did you like the story? Why or why not?

MATHEMATICS

# Symmetry

Complete each shape by drawing the mirror image.

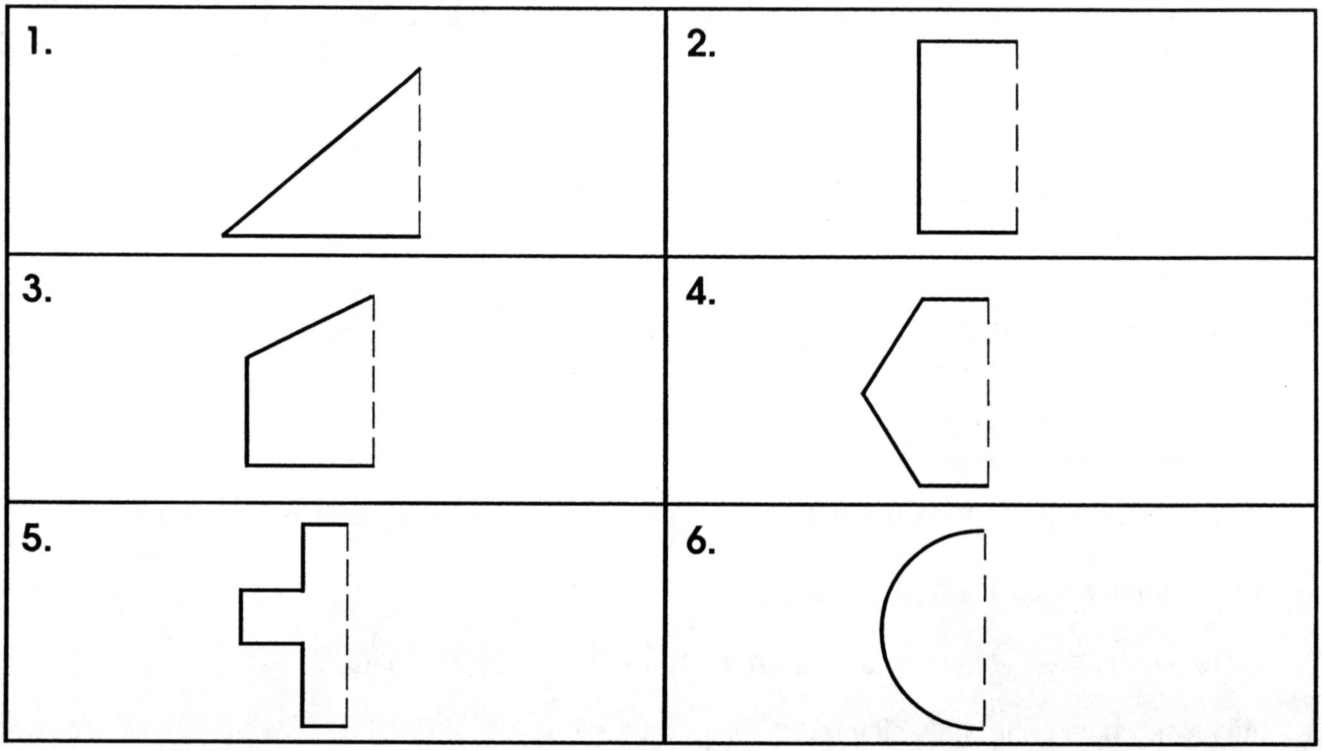


LANGUAGE

# Synonyms

A synonym is a word that has the **same meaning** as another word, such as "**nice**" and "**good**".

Write a synonym for each **underlined** word.

1. The king was a very **wealthy** man. ____________________
2. The horse galloped **quickly**. ____________________
3. **Sly** snakes can eat a whole frog. ____________________
4. They live in a **big** farmhouse in a rural town. ____________________
5. Commoners had **difficult** lives. ____________________
6. The queen had **beautiful** clothes. ____________________
7. Bears are **intelligent** animals. ____________________
8. Insects and **small** animals are near the bottom of the food chain.

____________________

# Simple Machines - Pulleys and Gears

A **pulley** is a wheel that changes the direction of a force. A pulley can reduce the force needed to move an object. An example of a pulley system is a well with a bucket on a rope.

A **gear** is a wheel with teeth. You can use gears to slow things down or speed them up, to change direction, or to control several things at once. An example of a gear can be found in a clock.

1. Circle the pictures that have a gear. **Underline** the pictures that have a pulley.

2. Look around your home and find examples of gears and pulleys.

   a) Things with gears:

   ______________________________________________

   ______________________________________________

   ______________________________________________

   b) Things with pulleys:

   ______________________________________________

   ______________________________________________

   ______________________________________________

MATHEMATICS

# Fractions

**1.** What fraction of these items have a ring around them?

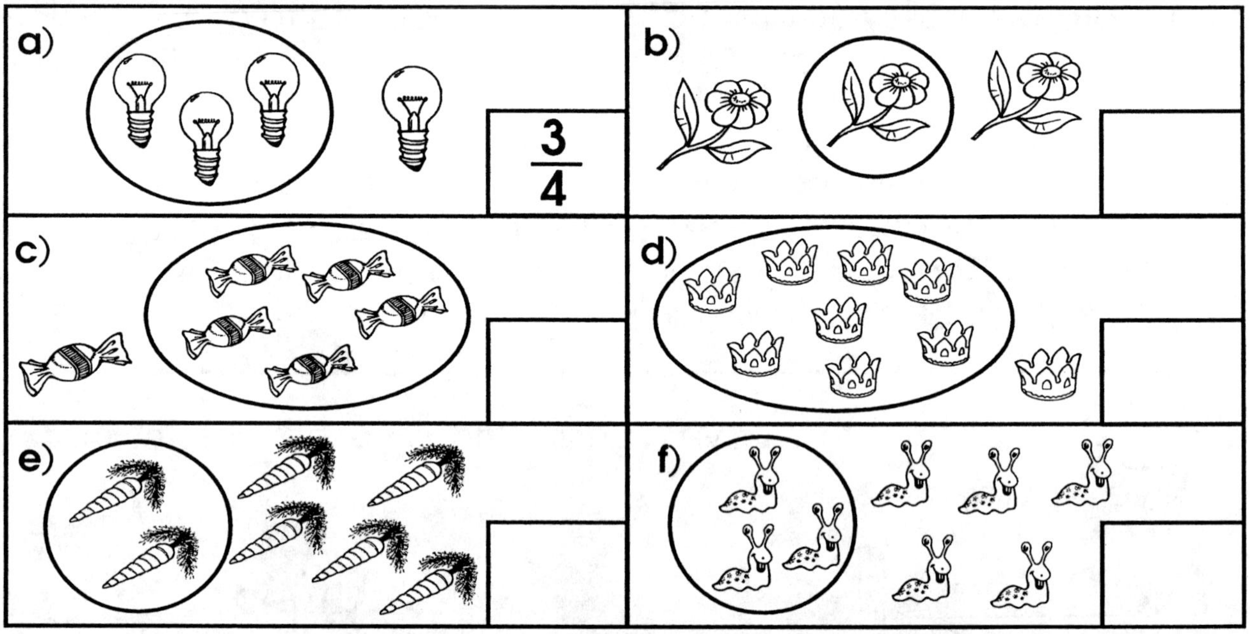


**2.** How much pizza is left? ____________

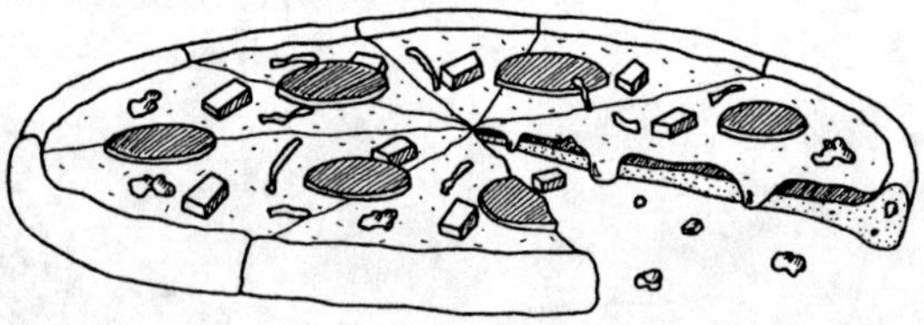

LANGUAGE

# Spelling

The **underlined** words are spelled wrong. On the line beside each incorrect word, write the correct spelling.

**Your hart** ____________ is **abowt** ____________ the size of your fist. **Feal** ____________ your pulse by **puting** ____________ two **fingurs** ____________ at the pulse points on your **nek** ____________ or wrists. You can feel the **blud** ____________ **stoping** ____________ and starting as it moves **insid** ____________ your arteries as the heart valves **opun** ____________ and **clothes** ____________. The largest artery in the **boddy** ____________ is the aorta. Capillaries **our** ____________ a network of small **toobs** ____________ throughout the body. In an average lifetime, your heart **wil** ____________ pump about one **milion** ____________ barrels of blood through your body!

# Common and Proper Nouns

LANGUAGE

A noun is a person, place or thing. There are two kinds of nouns. A **proper noun** is a specific person, place or thing (example: John). A **common noun** is a general person, place or thing (boy).

Circle the **proper** nouns. <u>**Underline**</u> the **common** nouns. Cross off the words that are **not** nouns.

**GIRL** **JENNIFER** **SUNDAY**

**CAKE** **FATHER**

**JUMP** **FRANCE** **HOSPITAL**

**DOLPHIN** **EMPTY**

**QUEEN VICTORIA** **SERVANT** **ALWAYS**

**HALLOWEEN** **DR. MALLOR**

# Counting Money

MATHEMATICS

How much money is shown in each box?

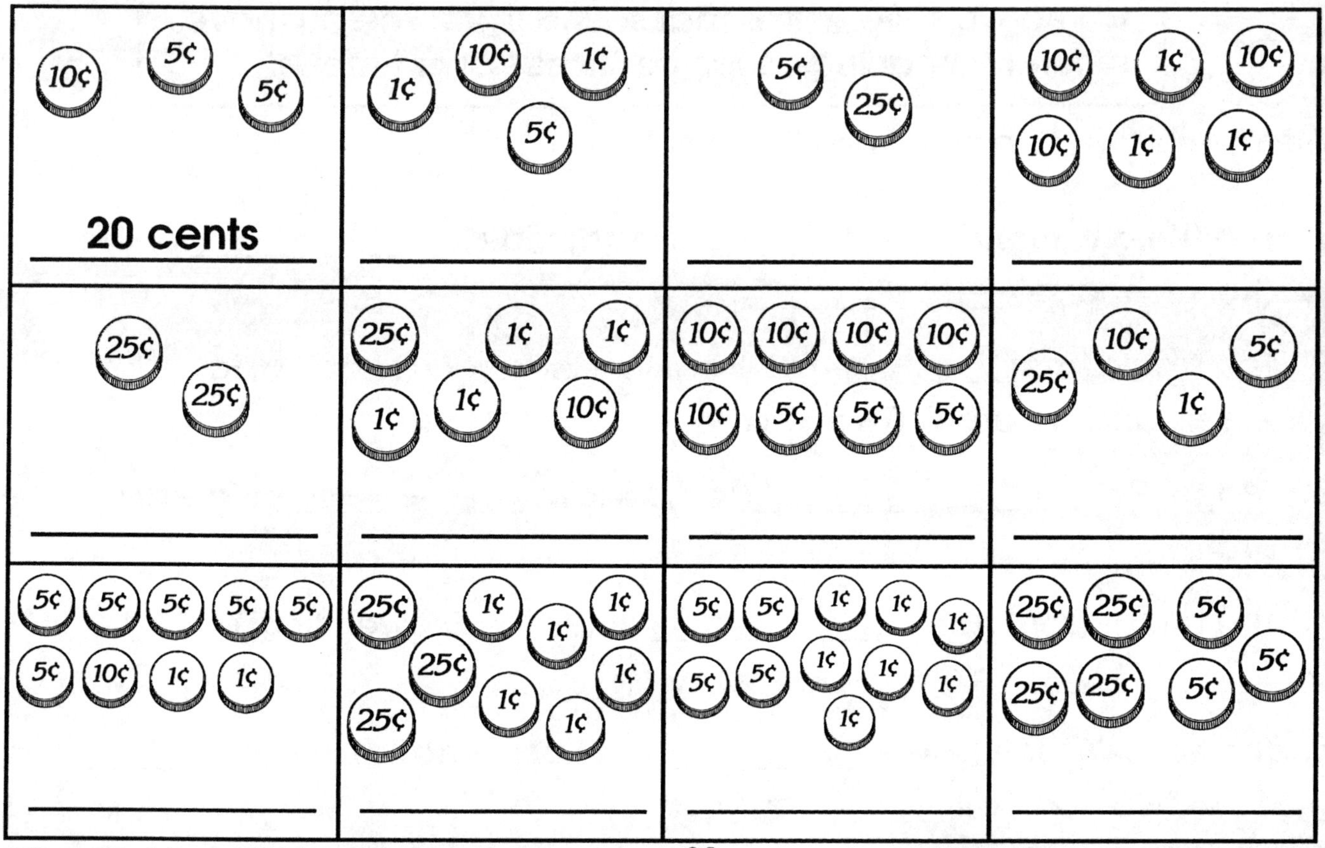

L A N G U A G E

## Subjects and Predicates

Every complete **sentence** contains two parts: a **subject** and a **predicate**. The subject is what (or who) the sentence is about, while the predicate tells something about the subject.

In each sentence about the medieval times below **circle** the **subject** and **underline** the **predicate**.

1. The knight was wounded in battle.
2. The chef prepared the king's dinner.
3. During Lent, they ate fish.
4. Rich families ate many kinds of food.
5. The king gave land to the nobles.
6. The lowest class of society were the peasants.

## Homonyms

Homonyms are words that **sound** the same but have, **different meanings**, such as "**nose**" and "**knows**".

Write the correct homonym in the blank.

1. The (**knight, night**) ______________ (**road, rode**) ______________ on his (**horse, hoarse**) ______________.
2. The (**male, mail**) ____________ carrier delivered (**two, too, to**) _______ letters and a parcel, (**two, too, to**) _______.
3. (**Page, Paige**) ______________ (**red, read**) ______________ a (**great, grate**) ______________ book.
4. The bright (**son, sun**) ______________ helps the (**flower, flour**) ______________ to grow.
5. The black (**bear, bare**) ______________ (**nose, knows**) ______________ how (**two, too, to**) ________ hunt.

## Problem Solving

MATHEMATICS

Using the prices of the items above, answer each question below in a complete sentence.

1. Paolo bought a hot dog, cookies and juice. How much did Paolo spend?

_______________________________________________

2. Alisha bought and sandwich and 2 drinks. How much did Alisha spend?

_______________________________________________

3. Jake bought 3 hot dogs. How much did Jake spend?

_______________________________________________

4. Janine bought a sandwich and cookies. How much did Janine spend?

_______________________________________________

## Sequencing Events - The Food Chain

Write the numbers one to five beside the sentences to show the order in which the events happen. Begin with one to show the bottom of the food chain.

_____ The snake eats the frog.

_____ The cricket eats the grass.

_____ The owl eats the snake.

_____ The sun shines on the grass.

_____ The frog eats the cricket.

READING

# Reading for Meaning

The royal family was seated around the large, wooden table. The room was **dim**, as the only light came from the candles at the center of the table. Delicious **aromas** of meat and sauces filled the air. Servants entered from the kitchen area with bowls of food. Plates and **cutlery** were not used. The king tore a piece of his bread from the loaf and hollowed out a dent in the middle of the chunk of bread. He then poured some sauce on the bread and set it on the table. He reached his **chubby** hand across to the chicken and ripped off a large piece of meat. After dipping the meat into the sauce, he hungrily held the meat to his mouth and bit into it. The servants stood nearby and waited to see if the family needed anything more. The king took a handful of carrots and ate those. When the meal was over, the king was **satisfied**.

1. Who is the main character? ______________________________

2. When do you think this story happened and why do you think it happened at that time? ______________________________

______________________________

3. How are the events in this story the same as your life? **How** are the events in this story different from your life?

______________________________

______________________________

4. Who else do you think may have been eating dinner?

______________________________

5. What do you think the following words mean?

dim - ______________________________

aromas - ______________________________

cutlery - ______________________________

chubby - ______________________________

satisfied - ______________________________

# Practice Drills

Add, subtract or multiply.

| | | | | | |
|---|---|---|---|---|---|
| a) 12 + 23 = ☐ | b) 24 - 14 = ☐ | c) 4 x 2 = ☐ | d) 902 - 321 = ☐ | e) 3 x 7 = ☐ | f) 27 + 65 = ☐ |
| g) 15 + ☐ = 19 | h) 6 x 3 = ☐ | i) 41 + 40 = ☐ | j) 634 - 515 = ☐ | k) 46 - ☐ = 23 | l) 5 x 5 = ☐ |
| m) 35 + 12 = ☐ | n) 72 - 23 = ☐ | o) 7 x 3 = ☐ | p) 234 - 142 = ☐ | q) 4 x 2 = ☐ | r) 93 + 41 = ☐ |
| s) 23 + ☐ = 30 | t) 3 x 3 = ☐ | u) 46 + 52 = ☐ | v) 634 - 330 = ☐ | w) 72 - ☐ = 70 | x) 8 x 2 = ☐ |

MATHEMATICS

# Using Verbs Correctly

Fill in the blanks using verbs that are given. For the first sentence, use the **present tense**. For the second sentence use the **past tense**.

1. **(to dive)**
   The otter ________________ under water to find plants and animals.
   The otter ________________ under water to find plants and animals.

2. **(to keep)**
   The polar bear's fur ________________ it warm while swimming.
   The polar bear's fur ________________ it warm while swimming.

3. **(to climb)**
   The bighorn sheep ________________ the steep mountain.
   The bighorn sheep ________________ the steep mountain.

4. **(to dig)**
   The baby weevil ________________ for underground roots.
   The baby weevil ________________ for underground roots.

LANGUAGE

# Writing a Letter

A proper **letter** must have a heading, greeting, body, closing and signature.

**Example:**

Mrs. J. Smith
3 Oak Drive
Miami, FL
23564 — **Heading**

**Greeting** — Dear Aunt Judy,

**Body** — Thank you for the birthday present. I love the book and I am on chapter three already!

I will see you at the wedding.

**Closing** — Love,

**Signature** — Katrina

On a separate piece of paper write a real letter to someone that you know. Ask an adult to help you mail it!

# Creative Writing

The medieval times were interesting times with many different **experiences than we have today. On a separate piece of paper, write** a story about this time period. Choose one to three **characters** (such as a king, peasant, servant or knight) and write a story about an adventure that they have. Include a lot of details and use interesting and creative ideas. Use adjectives and adverbs to describe how things **look and what is happening. After describing the setting** and the **main** character, tell about the **problem** that the character has. Then, show how the problem is **solved**. People who read your story will like it to have a happy ending.

Here are some examples of adjectives and adverbs that you may want to use in your story:

| | | | | |
|---|---|---|---|---|
| **handsome** | **charming** | **strong** | **courageously** | **angry** |
| **poor** | **homely** | **quickly** | **fancy** | **dirty** |
| **sleek** | **brave** | **huge** | **sturdy** | **quietly** |

# Answer Key

**Alphabetical Order: *(page 3)***
1. king, knight, nobleman, peasant, serf, viking
2. carnivore, decompser, ecosystem, food, herbivore, omnivore, predator
3. bakery, hospital, library, office, police, school, store, synagogue

**Addition and Subtraction Review: *(page 3)***

| | | | | |
|---|---|---|---|---|
| **a)** 78 | **b)** 90 | **c)** 72 | **d)** 26 | **e)** 11 |
| **f)** 479 | **g)** 889 | **h)** 899 | **i)** 111 | **j)** 210 |
| **k)** 335 | **l)** 500 | **m)** 51 | **n)** 661 | **o)** 92 |
| **p)** 771 | **q)** 1 023 | **r)** 972 | **s)** 299 | **t)** 809 |

**Root Words, Prefixes and Suffixes: *(page 4)***

| | | |
|---|---|---|
| **2.** might + y | **3.** early + er | **4.** un + happy |
| **5.** act + ion | **6.** re + tell | **7.** snore + ing |
| **8.** left + y | **9.** un + friend + ly | **10.** pretty + er |

**Sequencing Numbers: *(page 4)***
1. **a)** 9, 10, 11, 12, 13, 14, 15
   **b)** 74, 75, 76, 77, 78, 79, 80
   **c)** 127, 128, 129, 130, 131, 132
   **d)** 6 237, 6 238,6 239, 6 240, 6 241
   **e)** 1 098, 1 099, 1 100, 1 101, 1 102
2. **a)** 10, 9, 8, 7, 6, 5, 4
   **b)** 42, 41, 40, 39, 38, 37, 36
   **c)** 718, 717, 716, 715, 714, 713, 712
   **d)** 4 320, 4 319, 4 318, 4 317, 4 316
   **e)** 2 092, 2 091, 2 090, 2 089, 2 988

**The Medieval Times: *(page 5)***

**1.** b **2.** c **3.** d **4.** a

**Least to Greatest, Greatest to Least: *(page 6)***
1. **a)** 35, 45, 87, 92,
   **b)** 234, 344, 549, 602
   **c)** 106, 346, 756, 975
   **d)** 523, 564, 573, 590
   **e)** 210, 212, 216, 217
   **f)** 90, 85, 46, 45
   **g)** 934, 651, 547, 487
   **h)** 875, 734, 450, 231
   **i)** 690, 657, 651, 634
   **j)** 877, 875, 874, 870

**Prefixes and Suffixes: *(page 6)***

| | | | |
|---|---|---|---|
| **1.** unkind | **2.** friendliest | **3.** recall | **4.** longer |
| **5.** beautiful | **6.** unlucky | **7.** happier | **8.** reaction |
| **9.** memories | **10.** dislike | **11.** nicest | **12.** discussion |

**Addition - With an Unknown Term: *(page 7)***

| | | | |
|---|---|---|---|
| **b)** n = 10 | **c)** n = 8 | **d)** n = 14 | **e)** n = 5 |
| **f)** n = 13 | **g)** n = 11 | **h)** n = 10 | **i)** n = 12 |
| **j)** n = 13 | **k)** n = 8 | **l)** n = 12 | **m)** n = 10 |
| **n)** n = 11 | **o)** n = 14 | **p)** n = 11 | |

**Making Nouns Plural: *(page 7)***

| | | | |
|---|---|---|---|
| **1.** shelves | **2.** babies | **3.** foxes | **4.** children |
| **5.** mice | **6.** flies | **7.** leaves | **8.** berries |
| **9.** bushes | **10.** wolves | | |

**Reading for Understanding - The Food Chain: *(page 8)***
1. Plants need sunlight and water to grow.
2. Plants are important because everything else in the food chain either eats plants or eats things that eat plants.
3. herbivore; Answers may vary.
4. carnivores; Answers may vary.
5. meat, plants; Answers may vary.
6. A habitat is a community of plants and animals
7. Answers may vary.
8. Answers may vary; plants may have started growing there from seeds that were blown over by the wind or carried over by animals. Animals and insects are likely there looking for food and/or shelter.
9. Prey are animals that are hunted.
10. Answers may vary.
11. A predator is something that hunts other animals.
12. Answers may vary.
13. **a)** both **b)** predator **c)** both
    **d)** prey **e)** predator **f)** prey
14. All herbivores would die. Then, all omnivores and carnivores would die.

**Natural and Artificial Light: *(page 10)***
1. *Natural:* lightning, sun, stars
   *Artificial:* match, flashlight, candle, lightbulb, street lamp
2. *The following items should be circled:* candle, sun, flashlight, match, street lamp, lightbulb

**Greater Than or Less Than?: *(page 10)***

| | | |
|---|---|---|
| **b)** 45 < 67 | **c)** 80 > 34 | **d)** 21 < 78 |
| **e)** 75 < 76 | **f)** 84 > 48 | **g)** 123 < 678 |
| **h)** 787 < 877 | **i)** 934 < 943 | **j)** 344 < 400 |
| **k)** 810 < 890 | **l)** 378 < 387 | |

**Alliteration: *(page 11)***
Answers may vary.

**Subtraction - With and Without Regrouping: *(page 11)***

| | | | | |
|---|---|---|---|---|
| **a)** 29 | **b)** 39 | **c)** 59 | **d)** 18 | **e)** 38 |
| **f)** 117 | **g)** 379 | **h)** 197 | **i)** 411 | **j)** 209 |
| **k)** 129 | **l)** 209 | **m)** 128 | **n)** 148 | **o)** 76 |
| **p)** 188 | **q)** 506 | **r)** 489 | **s)** 556 | **t)** 476 |

**Characteristics of Plants: *(page 12)***
Answers may vary.

**Urban and Rural Communities: *(page 12)***
Answers may vary.

**Community Buildings: *(page 13)***
*Buildings circled:* hospital, airport, skyscraper
*Buildings boxed:* barn, house near mountains
*Buildings circled and boxed:* school, variety store, house with car

**Addition - With Units of Time: *(page 14)***

**b)** 9 hours 35 minutes **c)** 10 weeks
**d)** 3 weeks 6 days 11 hours 5 minutes

**Consonant Blends: *(page 14)***
Answers may vary.

**Multiplication Facts - 0 to 12: *(page 15)***

| X | 0 | 1 | 2 | 3 | 4 | 5 | 6 | 7 | 8 | 9 | 10 | 11 | 12 |
|---|---|---|---|---|---|---|---|---|---|---|---|---|---|
| **1** | 0 | 1 | 2 | 3 | 4 | 5 | 6 | 7 | 8 | 9 | **10** | 11 | 12 |
| **2** | 0 | **2** | 4 | 6 | 8 | 10 | 12 | 14 | 16 | 18 | 20 | 22 | 24 |
| **3** | 0 | 3 | 6 | 9 | 12 | 15 | 18 | 21 | 24 | 27 | 30 | 33 | 36 |
| **4** | 0 | 4 | 8 | 12 | 16 | 20 | 24 | 28 | 32 | 36 | 40 | 44 | 48 |
| **5** | 0 | 5 | 10 | 15 | 20 | **25** | 30 | 35 | 40 | 45 | 50 | 55 | 60 |
| **6** | 0 | 6 | 12 | 18 | 24 | 30 | 36 | 42 | 48 | 54 | 60 | 66 | 72 |
| **7** | **0** | 7 | 14 | 21 | 28 | 35 | 42 | 49 | 56 | 63 | 70 | 77 | 84 |
| **8** | 0 | 8 | 16 | 24 | 32 | 40 | 48 | 56 | 64 | 72 | 80 | 88 | 96 |
| **9** | 0 | 9 | 18 | 27 | 36 | 45 | 54 | 63 | 72 | 81 | 90 | 99 | 108 |
| **10** | 0 | 10 | 20 | **30** | 40 | 50 | 60 | 70 | 80 | 90 | 100 | 110 | 120 |
| **11** | 0 | 11 | 22 | 33 | 44 | 55 | 66 | 77 | **88** | 99 | 110 | 121 | 132 |
| **12** | 0 | 12 | 24 | 36 | 48 | 60 | 72 | 84 | 96 | 108 | 120 | 132 | 144 |

**Level of Sounds: *(page 15)***
*Items that should be circled:* gas lawnmower, loud scream, rock concert, space shuttle, many students talking in class

**Punctuation: *(page 16)***
1. There was a pyramid society. There were different classes of **people such as kings,** queens, lords, clerics and peasants.

2. Peasants worked long hours on farmland owned by a lord's manor. Men wore coarse tunics. Women wore long dresses of **coarse wool.**
3. She looked out the castle window and saw the knight, on his horse, charging directly towards the castle wall! Then, she **heard a big boom!**
4. The commoners' houses were made of cement, wood and straw.
5. "Ouch!" exclaimed the cook, as the boiling water splashed on **his arm.**
6. The king sniffed the plate of food placed before him and said, "Mmmm, this smells good!"

**More Multiplication:** ***(page 16)***

a) 12 b) 30 c) 20 d) 42 e) 40 f) 28
g) 18 h) 36 i) 6 j) 24 k) 18 l) 54
m) 56 n) 0 o) 24 p) 33 q) 20 r) 6
s) 27 t) 24 u) 4 v) 9 w) 15 x) 0
y) 72

**Contractions:** ***(page 17)***

1. They will 2. he is 3. king is 4. I would
5. could not 6. she will 7. you are 8. I am
9. Ian is 10. we have

**Possessive Pronouns:** ***(page 17)***

1. mine 2. his 3. their 4. our 5. his
6. Rupert's 7. its 8. your 9. my 10. her

**Growth and Changes in Plants:** ***(page 18)***

1. Answers may vary. 2. Answers may vary.
3. Answers may vary.
4. Fir tree should look the same in winter as in the summer. Apple tree should have bare branches (no leaves or apples) in the winter.

**More Punctuation:** ***(page 19)***

In medieval times, kings and queens lived in castles. Sometimes the enemy would attack the castle, so castles were often built on a mountain with a moat around it. A drawbridge lay across the moat to allow friends to get in, but the drawbridge would be raised if an **enemy came near.**

Castles had an inner wall and an outer wall. The outer wall was covered with merlons (steel plates). The walls were very thick to help prevent attackers from breaking them down. The walls had small slits called arrow loops. Defenders could shoot arrows at the enemy **through these slits.**

**Problem Solving:** ***(page 19)***

1. Each child got 5 cookies. 2. Each book cost $3.00.
3. They scored 2 runs in each inning.

**Identifying Verbs - Present and Past Tense:** ***(page 20)***

1. watched 2. is waiting 3. waited
4. invented 5. is 6. plays
7. swims, lunges

**Picture Division:** ***(page 20)***

Each predator should get:
a) 4 mice b) 2 rabbits c) 4 flies d) 3 fish

**Reading Comprehension:** ***(page 21)***

1. Roady Roadrunner 2. a desert at night
3. It is too hot to work or play. 4. roadrunner, snake, mouse, seeds
5. Realistic - this is how animals eat to survive.

**Book Report:** ***(page 21)***

Answers may vary.

**Symmetry:** ***(page 22)***

1. 2. 3. 4. 5. 6.

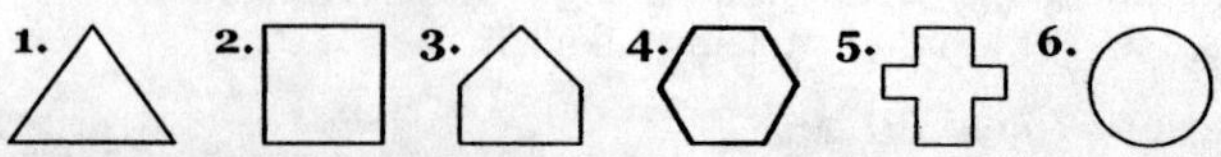

**Synonyms:** ***(page 22)***

Answers may vary.

**Simple Machines - Pulleys and Gears:** ***(page 23)***

1. *The following pictures should be circled:* watch, can opener, clock
   *The following pictures should be underlined:* clothesline, crane, well, flagpole
2. Answers may vary.

**Fractions:** ***(page 24)***

1. b) $\frac{1}{3}$ c) $\frac{5}{6}$ d) $\frac{8}{9}$ e) $\frac{2}{7}$ f) $\frac{3}{8}$
2. $\frac{7}{8}$

**Spelling:** ***(page 24)***

heart, about, Feel, putting, fingers, neck, blood, stopping, inside, open, close, body, are, tubes, will, million

**Common and Proper Nouns:** ***(page 25)***

*The following words should be circled:* JENNIFER, SUNDAY, FRANCE, QUEEN VICTORIA, HALLOWEEN, DR. MALLOR
*The following words should be underlined:* GIRL, CAKE, FATHER, HOSPITAL, DOLPHIN, SERVANT
*The following words should be crossed off:* JUMP, EMPTY, ALWAYS

**Counting Money:** ***(page 25)***

| | | | |
|---|---|---|---|
| 20 cents | 17 cents | 30 cents | 33 cents |
| 50 cents | 39 cents | 65 cents | 41 cents |
| 42 cents | 81 cents | 27 cents | 1 dollar 15 cents |

**Subjects and Predicates:** ***(page 26)***

1. knight — was wounded in battle
2. chef — prepared the king's dinner
3. they — During Lent, ate fish
4. Rich families — ate many kinds of food
5. king — gave land to the nobles
6. peasants — lowest class of society

**Homonyms:** ***(page 26)***

1. knight, rode, horse 2. mail, two, too
3. Paige, read, great 4. sun, flower
5. bear, knows, to

**Problem Solving:** ***(page 27)***

1. Paolo spent $3.50. 2. Alisha spent $4.00.
3. Jake spent $6.00. 4. Janine spent $4.00.

**Sequencing Events - The Food Chain:** ***(page 27)***

4 - The snake eats the frog. 2 - The cricket eats the grass.
5 - The owl eats the snake. 1- The sun shines on the grass.
3 - The frog eats the cricket.

**Reading for Meaning:** ***(page 28)***

1. the king
2. The story happens during the medieval times because, back then, people did not use cutlery and candles were used for light.
3. Answers may vary. 4. Answers may vary.
5. *dim* - not bright *aromas* - smells *cutlery* - eating utensils
   *chubby* - fat *satisfied* - happy

**Practice Drills:** ***(page 29)***

a) 35 b) 10 c) 8 d) 581 e) 21 f) 92 g) 4
h) 18 i) 81 j) 119 k) 23 l) 25 m) 47 n) 49
o) 21 p) 92 q) 8 r) 134 s) 7 t) 9 u) 98
v) 304 w) 2 x) 16

**Using Verbs Correctly:** ***(page 29)***

1. dives/dove 2. keeps/kept 3. climbs/climbed 4. digs/dug

**Writing a Letter:** ***(page 30)***

Answers may vary.

**Creative Writing:** ***(page 30)***

Answers may vary.

# Publication Listing



| Code # | Title and Grade |
|---|---|
| OTM-1114 | A Graph for all Seasons Gr. 1-3 |
| OTM-1492 | Abel's Island LL Gr. 4-6 |
| OTM-2504 | Addition Gr. 1-3 |
| OTM-1128 | Addition Drills Gr. 1-3 |
| OTM-1131 | Addition & Subtraction Drills Gr. 1-3 |
| OTM-14174 | Adv. of Huckle Berry Finn LL Gr. 7-8 |
| OTM-293 | All About Dinosaurs Gr. 2 |
| OTM-102 | All About Mexico Gr. 4-6 |
| OTM-120 | All About the Ocean Gr. 5-7 |
| OTM-249 | All About the Sea Gr. 4-6 |
| OTM-261 | All About Weather Gr. 7-8 |
| OTM-2110 | All Kinds of Structures Gr. 1 |
| OTM-601 | Amazing Aztecs Gr. 4-6 |
| OTM-1468 | Amelia Bedelia LL Gr. 1-3 |
| OTM-113 | America The Beautiful Gr. 4-6 |
| OTM-1457 | Amish Adventure LL Gr. 7-8 |
| OTM-602 | Ancient China Gr. 4-6 |
| OTM-618 | Ancient Egypt Gr. 4-6 |
| OTM-621 | Ancient Greece Gr. 4-6 |
| OTM-619 | Ancient Rome Gr. 4-6 |
| OTM-1453 | Anne of Green Gables LL Gr. 7-8 |
| OTM-1622 | Australia B/W Pictures |
| OTM-105 | Australia Gr. 5-8 |
| OTM-14224 | Banner in the Sky LL Gr. 7-8 |
| OTM-401 | Be Safe Not Sorry Gr. P-1 |
| OTM-1409 | Bear Tales in Literature Gr. 2-4 |
| OTM-14202 | Bears in Literature Gr. 1-3 |
| OTM-14257 | Because of Winn-Dixie LL Gr. 4-6 |
| OTM-1122 | Beginning Math Series: Measurement Gr. 1-3 |
| OTM-1119 | Beginning Math Series: Money Gr. 1-3 |
| OTM-1123 | Beginning Math Series: Numbers Gr. 1-3 |
| OTM-1108 | Beginning Math Series: Shapes Gr. 1-3 |
| OTM-1104 | Beginning Math Series: Calendar Gr. 2-3 |
| OTM-1110 | Beginning Math Series: Time Gr. 1-3 |
| OTM-1853 | Beginning Manuscript D.Gr. PK-2 |
| OTM-1854 | Beginning Cursive D. Gr. 2-4 |
| OTM-1857 | Beginning and Practice Manuscript D. Gr. PK-2 |
| OTM-1858 | Beginning and Practice Cursive D. Gr. 2-4 |
| OTM-1876 | Beginning Manuscript Z.B. Gr. PK-2 |
| OTM-1879 | Beginning Cursive Z.B. Gr. 2-4 |
| OTM-1882 | Beginning and Practice Cursive Z.B. Gr. 2-4 |
| OTM-1883 | Beginning and Practice Manuscript Z.B. Gr. PK-2 |
| OTM-14114 | Best Christmas Pageant Ever LL Gr. 4-6 |
| OTM-14107 | Borrowers, The LL Gr. 4-6 |
| OTM-1463 | Bridge to Terabithia LL Gr. 4-6 |
| OTM-2516 | BTS La Numeration/Numeration Gr. 1-3 |
| OTM-2517 | BTS L'addition/Addition Gr. 1-3 |
| OTM-2518 | BTS La Soustraction/ Subtraction Gr. 1-3 |
| OTM-2519 | BTS Les Sons/Phonics Gr. 1-3 |
| OTM-2520 | BTS La Comprehension de Textes/Reading for Meaning Gr. 1-3 |
| OTM-2521 | BTS Les Majuscules et la Ponctuation/ Cap. and Punctuation. Gr. 1-3 |
| OTM-2522 | BTS La Redaction de Phrases/ Sentence Writing Gr. 1-3 |
| OTM-2523 | BTS La Redaction de Textes/ Story Writing Gr. 1-3 |
| OTM-2524 | Numeración Gr. 1-3 |
| OTM-2525 | Adición Gr. 1-3 |
| OTM-2526 | Sustracción Gr. 1-3 |
| OTM-2527 | Fonética Gr. 1-3 |
| OTM-2528 | Leer para Entender Gr. 1-3 |
| OTM-2529 | Uso de las Mayúsculas y Reglas de Puntuación Gr. 1-3 |
| OTM-2530 | Composición de Oraciones Gr. 1-3 |
| OTM-2531 | Composici13n de Historias Gr. 1-3 |
| OTM-2513 | BTS Handwriting Manuscript D. Gr. 1-3 |
| OTM-2514 | BTS Handwriting Cursive D. Gr. 1-3 |
| OTM-2532 | BTS Handwriting Manuscript Z.B. Gr. 1-3 |
| OTM-2533 | BTS Handwriting Cursive Z.B. Gr. 1-3 |
| OTM-2515 | BTS Word Families Gr. 1-3 |
| OTM-14256 | Bud, Not Buddy LL Gr. 4-6 |
| OTM-1805 | Building Word Families #1 S.V. Gr. 1-2 |
| OTM-1807 | Building Word Families #2 L.V. Gr. 1-2 |
| OTM-14164 | Call It Courage LL Gr. 7-8 |
| OTM-1467 | Call of the Wild LL Gr. 7-8 |
| OTM-2507 | Capitalization & Punctuation Gr. 1-3 |
| OTM-14198 | Captain Courageous LL Gr. 7-8 |
| OTM-14154 | Castle in the Attic LL Gr. 4-6 |
| OTM-631 | Castles & Kings Reading Level 2-4 Gr. 4-6 |
| OTM-1434 | Cats in Literature Gr. 3-6 |
| OTM-14212 | Cay, The LL Gr. 7-8 |
| OTM-2107 | Cells, Tissues & Organs Gr. 7-8 |
| OTM-2101 | Characteristics of Flight Gr. 4-6 |
| OTM-1466 | Charlie and the Chocolate Factory LL Gr. 4-6 |
| OTM-1423 | Charlotte's Web LL Gr. 4-6 |
| OTM-109 | China Today Gr. 5-8 |
| OTM-1470 | Chocolate Fever LL Gr. 4-6 |
| OTM-14241 | Chocolate Touch LL Gr. 4-6 |
| OTM-14104 | Classical Poetry Gr. 7-12 |
| OTM-811 | Community Helpers Gr. 1-3 |
| OTM-14183 | Copper Sunrise NS Gr. 7-8 |
| OTM-1486 | Corduroy and Pocket for Corduroy LL Gr. 1-3 |
| OTM-234 | Creatures of the Sea Gr. 2-4 |
| OTM-14208 | Curse of the Viking Grave LL Gr. 7-8 |
| OTM-1121 | Data Management Gr. 4-6 |
| OTM-253 | Dealing with Dinosaurs Gr. 4-6 |
| OTM-14105 | Dicken's Christmas LL Gr. 7-8 |
| OTM-1621 | Dinosaurs B/W Pictures |
| OTM-216 | Dinosaurs Gr. 1 |
| OTM-298 | Dinosaurs Gr. 3 |
| OTM-14175 | Dinosaurs in Literature Gr. 1-3 |
| OTM-2106 | Diversity of Living Things Gr. 4-6 |
| OTM-1127 | Division Drills Gr. 4-6 |
| OTM-287 | Down by the Sea Gr. 1-3 |
| OTM-1416 | Dragons in Literature Gr. 3-6 |
| OTM-2109 | Earth's Crust Gr. 6-8 |
| OTM-1612 | Egypt B/W Pictures |
| OTM-14255 | Egypt Game LL Gr. 4-6 |
| OTM-628 | Egyptians Today and Yesterday Gr. 2-3 |
| OTM-2108 | Electricity Gr. 4-6 |
| OTM-285 | Energy: The World & You Gr. 4-6 |
| OTM-2123 | Environment, The Gr. 4-6 |
| OTM-1812 | ESL Teaching Ideas Gr. K-8 |
| OTM-14258 | Esperanza Rising NS Gr. 4-6 |
| OTM-1822 | Exercises in Grammar Gr. 6 |
| OTM-1823 | Exercises in Grammar Gr. 7 |
| OTM-1824 | Exercises in Grammar Gr. 8 |
| OTM-1054 | Exploring Canada Gr. 1-3 |
| OTM-1056 | Exploring Canada Gr. 1-6 |
| OTM-1055 | Exploring Canada Gr. 4-6 |
| OTM-820 | Exploring My School and Community Gr. 1 |
| OTM-1415 | Fables Gr. 4-6 |
| OTM-1639 | Fables B/W Pictures |
| OTM-14210 | Fantastic Mr. Fox LL Gr. 4-6 |
| OTM-14168 | First 100 Sight Words Gr. 1 |
| OTM-14261 | Flat Stanley LL Gr. 1-3 |
| OTM-14170 | Flowers for Algernon LL Gr. 7-8 |
| OTM-14128 | Fly Away Home LL Gr. 4-6 |
| OTM-405 | Food: Fact, Fun & Fiction Gr. 1-3 |
| OTM-406 | Food: Nutrition & Invention Gr. 4-6 |
| OTM-2118 | Force and Motion Gr. 1-3 |
| OTM-2119 | Force and Motion Gr. 4-6 |
| OTM-14263 | Fractured Fairy Tales LL Gr. 1-3 |
| OTM-14172 | Freckle Juice LL Gr. 1-3 |
| OTM-14260 | Frindle LL Gr. 4-6 |
| OTM-1849 | Fun with Phonics Gr. 1-3 |
| OTM-14209 | Giver, The LL Gr. 7-8 |
| OTM-1490 | Great Expectations LL Gr. 7-8 |
| OTM-14169 | Great Gilly Hopkins LL Gr. 4-6 |
| OTM-14238 | Greek Mythology Gr. 7-8 |
| OTM-2113 | Growth and Change in Animals Gr. 2-3 |
| OTM-2114 | Growth and Change in Plants Gr. 2-3 |
| OTM-2104 | Habitats Gr. 4-6 |
| OTM-14205 | Harper Moon LL Gr. 7-8 |
| OTM-14136 | Hatchet LL Gr. 7-8 |
| OTM-14184 | Hobbit LL Gr. 7-8 |
| OTM-14250 | Holes LL Gr. 4-6 |
| OTM-14133 | How To Eat Fried Worms LL 4-6 |
| OTM-1848 | How To Give a Presentation Gr. 4-6 |
| OTM-14125 | How To Teach Writing Through Gr. 7-9 |
| OTM-1810 | How To Write a Composition Gr. 6-10 |
| OTM-1809 | How To Write a Paragraph Gr. 5-10 |
| OTM-1808 | How To Write an Essay Gr. 7-12 |
| OTM-1803 | How To Write Poetry and Stories Gr. 4-6 |
| OTM-407 | Human Body Gr. 2-4 |
| OTM-402 | Human Body Gr. 4-6 |
| OTM-605 | In Days of Yore Gr. 4-6 |
| OTM-606 | In Pioneer Days Gr. 2-4 |
| OTM-241 | Incredible Dinosaurs Gr. P-1 |
| OTM-14177 | Incredible Journey LL Gr. 4-6 |
| OTM-14100 | Indian in the Cupboard LL Gr. 4-6 |
| OTM-14193 | Island of the Blue Dolphins LL 4-6 |
| OTM-1465 | James & The Giant Peach LL 4-6 |
| OTM-1625 | Japan B/W Pictures |
| OTM-106 | Japan Gr. 5-8 |
| OTM-14264 | Journey to the Center of the Earth LL Gr. 7-8 |
| OTM-1461 | Julie of the Wolves NS Gr. 7-8 |
| OTM-502 | Junior Music for Fall Gr. 4-6 |
| OTM-505 | Junior Music for Spring Gr. 4-6 |
| OTM-506 | Junior Music Made Easy for Winter Gr. 4-6 |
| OTM-1862 | Just for Boys – Reading Composition Gr 3-6 |
| OTM-1863 | Just for Boys – Reading Composition Gr. 6-8 |
| OTM-1450 | Legends Gr. 4-6 |
| OTM-14130 | Life & Adv. of Santa Claus LL 7-8 |
| OTM-210 | Life in a Pond Gr. 3-4 |
| OTM-630 | Life in the Middle Ages Gr. 7-8 |
| OTM-2103 | Light & Sound Gr. 4-6 |
| OTM-14219 | Light in the Forest LL Gr. 7-8 |
| OTM-1446 | Lion, Witch and the Wardrobe LL Gr. 4-6 |
| OTM-1851 | Literature Response Forms Gr. 1-3 |
| OTM-1852 | Literature Response Forms Gr. 4-6 |
| OTM-14233 | Little House on the Prairie LL 4-6 |
| OTM-14269 | Loser LL Gr. 4-6 |
| OTM-14109 | Lost in the Barrens LL Gr. 7-8 |
| OTM-278 | Magnets Gr. 3-5 |
| OTM-403 | Making Sense of Our Senses K-1 |
| OTM-294 | Mammals Gr. 1 |
| OTM-295 | Mammals Gr. 2 |
| OTM-296 | Mammals Gr. 3-4 |
| OTM-297 | Mammals Gr. 5-6 |
| OTM-14160 | Maniac Magee LL Gr. 4-6 |
| OTM-119 | Mapping Activities & Outlines! 4-8 |
| OTM-117 | Mapping Skills Gr. 1-3 |
| OTM-107 | Mapping Skills Gr. 4-6 |
| OTM-2116 | Matter & Materials Gr. 1-3 |
| OTM-2117 | Matter & Materials Gr. 4-6 |
| OTM-1116 | Measurement Gr. 4-8 |
| OTM-1609 | Medieval Life B/W Pictures |
| OTM-270 | Microscopy Gr. 5-8 |
| OTM-1413 | Mice in Literature Gr. 3-5 |
| OTM-14180 | Midnight Fox LL Gr. 4-6 |
| OTM-14266 | Missing May LL Gr. 4-6 |
| OTM-1118 | Money Talks Gr. 3-6 |
| OTM-1443 | Monkeys in Literature Gr. 2-4 |
| OTM-1497 | Mouse & the Motorcycle LL 4-6 |
| OTM-1494 | Mr. Poppers Penguins LL Gr. 4-6 |
| OTM-14201 | Mrs. Frisby & Rats LL Gr. 4-6 |
| OTM-1826 | Multi-Level Spelling USA Gr. 3-6 |
| OTM-1132 | Multiplication & Division Drills 4-6 |
| OTM-1130 | Multiplication Drills Gr. 4-6 |
| OTM-114 | My Country! The USA! Gr. 2-4 |
| OTM-1437 | Mystery at Blackrock Island LL 7-8 |
| OTM-14157 | Nate the Great and Sticky Case LL Gr. 1-3 |
| OTM-110 | New Zealand Gr. 4-8 |
| OTM-1475 | Novel Ideas Gr. 4-6 |
| OTM-14244 | Number the Stars LL Gr. 4-6 |
| OTM-2503 | Numeration Gr. 1-3 |
| OTM-1459 | On the Banks of Plum Creek LL Gr. 4-6 |
| OTM-14220 | One In the Middle Is Green Kangaroo LL Gr. 1-3 |
| OTM-272 | Our Trash Gr. 2-3 |
| OTM-2121 | Our Universe Gr. 5-8 |
| OTM-286 | Outer Space Gr. 1-2 |
| OTM-118 | Outline Maps of the World Gr. 1-8 |
| OTM-1431 | Owls in the Family LL Gr. 4-6 |
| OTM-1452 | Paperbag Princess LL Gr. 1-3 |
| OTM-212 | Passport to Australia Gr. 4-5 |
| OTM-1804 | Personal Spelling Dictionary Gr. 2-5 |
| OTM-503 | Phantom of the Opera Gr. 6-9 |
| OTM-2506 | Phonics Gr. 1-3 |
| OTM-1133 | Picture Book Math Gr. 1-3 |
| OTM-1448 | Pigs in Literature Gr. 2-4 |
| OTM-1499 | Pinballs LL Gr. 4-6 |
| OTM-634 | Pirates Gr. 4-6 |
| OTM-2120 | Planets Gr. 3-6 |
| OTM-1874 | Poetry Prompts Gr. 1-3 |
| OTM-1875 | Poetry Prompts Gr. 4-6 |
| OTM-624 | Prehistoric Times Gr. 4-6 |
| OTM-1855 | Practice Manuscript D. Gr. PK-2 |
| OTM-1856 | Practice Cursive D. Gr. 2-4 |
| OTM-1880 | Practice Manuscript Z.B. Gr. PK-2 |
| OTM-1881 | Practice Cursive Z.B. Gr. 2-4 |
| OTM-501 | Primary Music for Fall Gr. 1-3 |
| OTM-504 | Primary Music for Spring Gr. 4-6 |
| OTM-507 | Primary Music for Winter Gr. 1-3 |
| OTM-14262 | Prince Caspian LL Gr. 4-6 |
| OTM-1120 | Probability and Inheritance Gr. 7-10 |
| OTM-1426 | Rabbits in Literature Gr. 2-4 |
| OTM-1444 | Ramona Quimby Age 8 LL 4-6 |
| OTM-2508 | Reading for Meaning Gr. 1-3 |
| OTM-1876 | Reading Logs Gr. K-1 |
| OTM-1877 | Reading Logs Gr. 2-3 |
| OTM-14162 | Reading with Arnold Lobel Gr. 2-3 |
| OTM-14234 | Reading with Arthur Gr. 1-3 |
| OTM-1440 | Reading with Beatrix Potter 2-4 |
| OTM-14129 | Reading with Beatrix Potter: Biography Gr. 2-4 |
| OTM-14200 | Reading with Curious George Gr. 2-4 |
| OTM-14230 | Reading with Eric Carle Gr. 1-3 |
| OTM-14126 | Reading with Franklin Gr. 1-3 |
| OTM-14251 | Reading with Kenneth Oppel 4-6 |
| OTM-1427 | Reading with Mercer Mayer 1-2 |
| OTM-14171 | Reading with Phoebe Gilman Gr. 2-3 |
| OTM-14142 | Reading with Robert Munsch Gr. 1-3 |
| OTM-14140 | Reading with Kids at Bailey Elem. School Gr. 2-4 |
| OTM-14167 | Reading with Magic School Bus Gr. 1-3 |
| OTM-14247 | Reading with Magic Treehouse Gr. 1-3 |
| OTM-14225 | River, The LL Gr. 7-8 |
| OTM-508 | Robert Schumann-Life & Times Gr. 6-9 |
| OTM-265 | Rocks & Minerals Gr. 4-6 |
| OTM-269 | Rocks & Soils Gr. 2-3 |
| OTM-14103 | Sadako and 1 000 Paper Cranes LL Gr. 4-6 |
| OTM-404 | Safety Gr. 2-4 |
| OTM-1442 | Sarah Plain & Tall LL Gr. 4-6 |
| OTM-1601 | Sea Creatures B/W Pictures |
| OTM-279 | Sea Creatures Gr. 1-3 |
| OTM-1464 | Secret Garden LL Gr. 4-6 |
| OTM-2502 | Sentence Writing Gr. 1-3 |
| OTM-1430 | Serendipity Series Gr. 3-5 |
| OTM-1866 | Shakespeare Shorts – Performing Arts Gr. 2-4 |
| OTM-1867 | Shakespeare Shorts – Performing Arts Gr. 4-6 |
| OTM-1868 | Shakespeare Shorts – Language Arts Gr. 2-4 |
| OTM-1869 | Shakespeare Shorts – Language Arts Gr. 4-6 |
| OTM-14158 | Shilo LL Gr. 4-6 |
| OTM-14181 | Sight Word Activities Gr. 1 |
| OTM-2100 | Simple Machines Gr. 1-3 |
| OTM-299 | Simple Machines Gr. 4-6 |
| OTM-2122 | Solar System Gr. 4-6 |
| OTM-111 | South American Countries Gr. 4-6 |
| OTM-1644 | South American B/W Pictures |

# Publication Listing

| Code # | Title and Grade |
|---|---|
| OTM-205 | Space Gr. 2-3 |
| OTM-1814 | Spelling Gr. 1 |
| OTM-1815 | Spelling Gr. 2 |
| OTM-1816 | Spelling Gr. 3 |
| OTM-1817 | Spelling Gr. 4 |
| OTM-1818 | Spelling Gr. 5 |
| OTM-1819 | Spelling Gr. 6 |
| OTM-1834 | Spelling Blacklines Gr. 1 |
| OTM-1835 | Spelling Blacklines Gr. 2 |
| OTM-1836 | Spelling Blacklines Gr. 3 |
| OTM-1837 | Spelling Blacklines Gr. 4 |
| OTM-1827 | Spelling Worksavers #1 Gr. 3-5 |
| OTM-2125 | Stable Structures & Mech. Gr. 3 |
| OTM-14139 | Stone Fox LL Gr. 4-6 |
| OTM-14214 | Stone Orchard LL Gr. 7-8 |
| OTM-1864 | Story Starters Gr. 1-3 |
| OTM-1865 | Story Starters Gr. 4-6 |
| OTM-1873 | Story Starters Gr. 1-6 |
| OTM-2509 | Story Writing Gr. 1-3 |
| OTM-2111 | Structures, Mechanisms & Motion Gr. 2 |
| OTM-14211 | Stuart Little LL Gr. 4-6 |
| OTM-2505 | Subtraction Gr. 1-3 |
| OTM-1129 | Subtraction Drills Gr. 1-3 |
| OTM-2511 | Successful Language Practice Gr. 1-3 |
| OTM-2512 | Successful Math Practice Gr. 1-3 |
| OTM-2309 | Summer Learning Gr. K-1 |
| OTM-2310 | Summer Learning Gr. 1-2 |
| OTM-2311 | Summer Learning Gr. 2-3 |
| OTM-2312 | Summer Learning Gr. 3-4 |
| OTM-2313 | Summer Learning Gr. 4-5 |
| OTM-2314 | Summer Learning Gr. 5-6 |
| OTM-14159 | Summer of the Swans LL Gr. 4-6 |
| OTM-1418 | Superfudge LL Gr. 4-6 |
| OTM-108 | Switzerland Gr. 4-6 |
| OTM-115 | Take a Trip to Australia Gr. 2-3 |
| OTM-2102 | Taking Off With Flight Gr. 1-3 |
| OTM-1455 | Tales of the Fourth Grade LL 4-6 |
| OTM-1135 | Teaching Math Through Sports Gr. 5-8 |
| OTM-1134 | Teaching Math with Everyday Manipulatives Gr. 4-6 |
| OTM-14265 | The Breadwinner LL Gr. 4-6 |
| OTM-14259 | The Tale of Despereaux LL Gr. 4-6 |
| OTM-1472 | Ticket to Curlew LL Gr. 4-6 |
| OTM-14222 | To Kill a Mockingbird LL Gr. 7-8 |
| OTM-14163 | Traditional Poetry Gr. 7-10 |
| OTM-1481 | Tuck Everlasting LL Gr. 4-6 |
| OTM-14126 | Turtles in Literature Gr. 1-3 |
| OTM-1427 | Unicorns in Literature Gr. 3-5 |
| OTM-617 | Viking Age, The Gr. 4-6 |
| OTM-14206 | War with Grandpa LL Gr. 4-6 |
| OTM-2124 | Water Gr. 2-4 |
| OTM-260 | Weather Gr. 4-6 |
| OTM-1417 | Wee Folk in Literature Gr. 3-5 |
| OTM-808 | What is a Community? Gr. 2-4 |
| OTM-262 | What is the Weather Today? 2-4 |
| OTM-1473 | Where the Red Fern Grows LL Gr. 7-8 |
| OTM-1487 | Where the Wild Things Are LL Gr. 1-3 |
| OTM-14187 | Whipping Boy LL Gr. 4-6 |
| OTM-14226 | Who is Frances Rain? LL Gr. 4-6 |
| OTM-509 | Wolfgang Amadeus Mozart Gr. 6-9 |
| OTM-14213 | Wolf Island LL Gr. 1-3 |
| OTM-1859 | Word Families 2, 3 Letter Words Gr. 1-3 |
| OTM-1860 | Word Families 3, 4 Letter Words Gr. 1-3 |
| OTM-1861 | Word Families 2, 3, 4 Letter Words Big Book Gr. 1-3 |
| OTM-620 | World Explorers Gr. 4-6 |
| OTM-14221 | Wrinkle in Time LL Gr. 7-8 |

| Code # | Title and Grade |
|---|---|

| Code # | Title and Grade |
|---|---|

| Code # | Title and Grade |
|---|---|